ISBN 978-0-282-78258-0
PIBN 10864348

1 MONTH OF
FREE
READING

at
www.ForgottenBooks.com

By purchasing this book you are
eligible for one month membership to
ForgottenBooks.com, giving you
unlimited access to our entire
collection of over 1,000,000 titles via
our web site and mobile apps.

To claim your free month visit:
www.forgottenbooks.com/free864348

Of this edition 950 copies were printed,
including 30 copies on Japan vellum.

DEFINITION
OF A GENTLEMAN

By CARDINAL NEWMAN

THE KIRGATE PRESS
LEWIS BUDDY 3rd
AT 'HILLSIDE' IN CANTON
PENNSYLVANIA
MCM & I

25051
^03

THE DEFINITION OF
A GENTLEMAN

✠

IT is almost a definition of a gentleman to say that he is one who never inflicts pain. This description is both refined and, so far as it goes, accurate. He is mainly occupied in merely removing the obstacles which hinder the free and unembar‚ rassed action of those about him, and he concurs with their movements rather than takes the initiative himself. His ben‚ efits may be considered as par‚

allel to what are called the comforts or conveniences in arrangements of a personal nature — like an easy chair or a good fire, which do their best in dispelling cold and fatigue, though nature provides both means of rest and animal heat without them. The true gentleman in like manner carefully avoids whatever may cause a jar or a jolt in the mind of those with whom he is cast — all clashing of opinion or collision of feeling, all restraint or suspicion or gloom or resentment, his great concern being to make every one at ease and at home. He has his eyes on all his company, he is tender towards the bashful, gentle towards the distant, and merciful towards the absurd. He can recollect to whom he is speaking; he guards against unseasonable allusions or topics which may irritate; he is seldom prominent in conversation, and never wearisome. He makes light of favors when he does them, and seems to be receiving when he is conferring. He never speaks of himself except when compelled, never defends himself by a mere retort; he has no ears for slander or gossip, is scrupu-

lous in imputing motives to those who interfere with him, and interprets everything for the best. He is never mean or little in his disputes, never takes unfair advantage, never mistakes personalities or sharp sayings for arguments, or insinuates evil which he dare not say out. From a long-sighted prudency, he observes the maxim of the ancient sage, that we should ever conduct ourselves towards our enemy as if he were one day to be our friend. He has too much good sense to be affronted at insults. He is too well employed to re-

member injuries and too indo-
lent to bear malice. He is pa-
tient, forbearing, and resigned
on philosophical principle; he
submits to pain because it is
inevitable, to bereavement because it is irreparable, and to
death because it is his destiny.
If he engages in controversy of
any kind, his disciplined intellect preserves him from the
blundering discourtesy of bet-
ter, perhaps, but less educated
minds, who, like blunt weapons,
tear and hack instead of cutting
clean, who mistake the point in
argument, waste their strength
on trifles, misconceive their

adversary, and leave the question more involved than they find it. He may be right or wrong in his opinion, but he is too clear-headed to be unjust; he is as simple as he is forcible, and as brief as he is decisive. Nowhere shall we find greater candor, consideration, indulgence; he throws himself into the minds of his opponents, he accounts for their mistakes. He knows the weakness of human reason as well as its strength, its province, and its limits. If he be an unbeliever, he will be too profound and large-minded to ridicule religion or to act against it; he is too wise to be a dogmatist or fanatic in his infidelity. He respects piety and devotion; he even supports institutions as venerable, beau, tiful, or useful, to which he does not assent; he honors the min, isters of religion, and it contents him to decline its mysteries without assailing or denounc, ing them. He is a friend of re, ligious toleration, and that not only because his philosophy has taught him to look on all forms of faith with an impartial eye, but also from the gentle, ness and effeminacy of feeling which is the attendant on civili,

zation. Not that he may not hold a religion, too, in his own way, even when he is not a Christian. In that case his religion is one of imagination and sentiment; it is the embodiment of those ideas of the sublime, majestic, and beautiful without which there can be no large philosophy. Sometimes he acknowledges the being of God, sometimes he invests an unknown principle or qualities with the attributes of perfection. And this deduction of his reason or creation of his fancy he makes the occasion of such excellent thoughts, and the starting-point of so varied and systematic a teaching, that he even seems like a disciple of Christianity itself. From the very accuracy and steadiness of his logical powers, he is able to see what sentiments are consistent in those who hold any religious doctrine at all, and he appears to others to feel and to hold a whole circle of theological truths, which exist in his mind otherwise than as a number of deductions. Such are some of the lineaments of the ethical character which the cultivated intellect will form, apart from the religious principle.

They are seen within the pale of the church and without it, in holy men and in profligate; they form the beau-ideal of the world; they partly assist and partly distort the development of the Catholic. They may sub-serve the education of a St. Francis de Sales or a Cardinal Pole; they may be the limits of contemplations of a Shaftes-bury or a Gibbon. Basil and Julian were fellow-students at the schools of Athens; and one became the saint and doctor of the Church, the other a scoff-ing and relentless foe.

Made in the USA
Columbia, SC
28 April 2024

35009462R00020